Brazil Safari

by Grace Hansen

Abdo Kids Jumbo is an Imprint of Abdo Kids
abdobooks.com

abdobooks.com

Published by Abdo Kids, a division of ABDO, P.O. Box 398166, Minneapolis, Minnesota 55439.

Printed in the United States of America, North Mankato, Minnesota.

052024

092024

THIS BOOK CONTAINS RECYCLED MATERIALS

Photo Credits: Getty Images, Shutterstock

Production Contributors: Teddy Borth, Jennie Forsberg, Grace Hansen
Design Contributors: Victoria Bates, Candice Keimig

Library of Congress Control Number: 2023948664

Publisher's Cataloging-in-Publication Data

Names: Hansen, Grace, author.

Title: Brazil safari / by Grace Hansen

Description: Minneapolis, Minnesota : Abdo Kids, 2025 | Series: World safaris | Includes online resources and index.

Identifiers: ISBN 9798384900818 (lib. bdg.) | ISBN 9798384901518 (ebook) | ISBN 9798384901860 (Read-to-me eBook)

Subjects: LCSH: Safaris--Juvenile literature. | Natural areas--Juvenile literature. | Brazil--Description and travel--Juvenile literature. | Wilderness areas--Juvenile literature. | Travel--Juvenile literature.

Classification: DDC 981--dc23

Table of Contents

Let's Go on Safari!

Brazil is a country in South America. It is home to large parts of the Amazon River and rainforest. These places are filled with amazing animals. Let's go on safari in Brazil!

Amazon River
Amazon Rainforest
Brazil
South America

A safari is a tour where people can see wild animals in their **habitats**. There are many ways to go on safari in Brazil. Some people go by foot or by Jeep. Others go on safari by boat.

60
60

Amazon Animals

In the Amazon River, giant otters swim and hunt. They are easy to spot since they reach 5 feet (1.5 m) in length!

Even larger are Amazon river dolphins. River dolphins are toothed whales. Adults are pale pink in color.

Black caimans are the largest reptiles in the Amazon **basin**. They can be found along freshwater **habitats**.

South American tapirs are the largest **native** land animal in the Amazon. They are very good swimmers. They can be seen in water using their long noses to help them breathe.

On land, giant armadillos spend their days resting in **burrows**. They come out at night in search of **termites**, ants, and worms to eat.

Jaguars are known for being excellent swimmers and climbers. The best places to spot them is on riverbanks or in trees where they hunt and eat.

Toco toucans spend their days eating fruit in trees. Their bright **bills** are easy to see. People can listen for the noises they make, such as croaking and barking.

Brazil Safari Experiences

Explore Cave Formations
Blue Lake Grotto, Bonito

Go Horseback Riding
Pantanal Wetlands

Kayak through the Flooded Forest
Igapó

Swim with Tropical Fish
Jericoacoara

Glossary

basin – a large area of land drained by a river.

bill – the parts of a bird's jaw that form the beak.

burrow – a hole or tunnel dug by certain animals for use as a hiding place or home.

habitat – the natural environment of a plant or animal.

native – an animal naturally found in a given place.

termite – an insect that looks somewhat like an ant, lives in large groups, and eats wood.

Index